INTRODUCTION

THE STORY OF AMERICA echoes with drama and with action. It is a rousing tale of personal valor and political accomplishment, one that began with an unquenchable yearning for liberty among a small group of dedicated patriots. That yearning soon led men such as George Washington and Thomas Jefferson to proclaim the formation of a new nation based on the principles of freedom and justice for all.

The establishment of the fledgling United States of America came at the price of a long and bloody war with England. Even following the American triumph in the Revolution, difficulties lay ahead. A working government had to be created to bind together the sometimes fractious colonies. A permanent capital had to be chosen and built. Another war with England would be fought in 1812. Later, internal strains within the growing republic would lead to the catastrophe of civil war.

Despite such trials, the nation endured, buoyed by the efforts of its courageous leaders. Indeed, the nation flourished, growing from the original 13 Atlantic colonies to a country that spanned a continent. Free enterprise proved to be a cornerstone of the country's success. Sparked by competition, innovation followed innovation in business and in industry, transforming the United States into a world economic power.

To foster a greater awareness and appreciation of this nation's stirring past is a goal shared by the National Society of the Daughters of the American Revolution and the United States Capitol Historical Society. This book represents a project sponsored jointly by the two organizations—the recording of the American story in art. Fittingly, the story is presented in the U.S. Capitol itself, captured in a series of murals that grace the corridors of the House wing.

Painted between 1973 and 1982, the murals feature 24 major historical scenes accompanied by paintings of the early meeting places of Congress and numerous portraits of important figures in and out of government. Their creator was the noted muralist Allyn Cox. The resounding success of his efforts is evident to all who study these paintings, either firsthand or in the pages that follow. It is the hope of the Daughters of the American Revolution and the U.S. Capitol Historical Society that Mr. Cox's work may help perpetuate the rich historical legacy of our nation.

PLANNING AND PAINTING THE HOUSE WING MURALS

Allyn Cox completes a scene in the Hall of Capitols, the first of two House wing corridors painted by the artist from 1973 to 1982.

ALLYN COX WAS EMINENTLY QUALIFIED for his work in the U.S. Capitol. Born in 1896, he was the son of two accomplished artists, Kenyon and Louise Howland King Cox. Trained in the United States and in Italy, Cox steadily built his reputation as a muralist over many years. He was originally called to the Capitol in 1953 to complete the series of paintings on the Rotunda frieze begun by Constantino Brumidi, the 19th-century artist who labored for a quarter-century beautifying the halls of government. The 32-foot section painted by Cox depicts scenes of the Civil War, the Spanish-American War, and the birth of aviation at Kitty Hawk, North Carolina. Cox later painted a portrait of Henry Clay in the Senate Reception Room and recorded man's

THE AMERICAN STORY IN ART

THE MURALS OF ALLYN COX IN THE U.S. CAPITOL

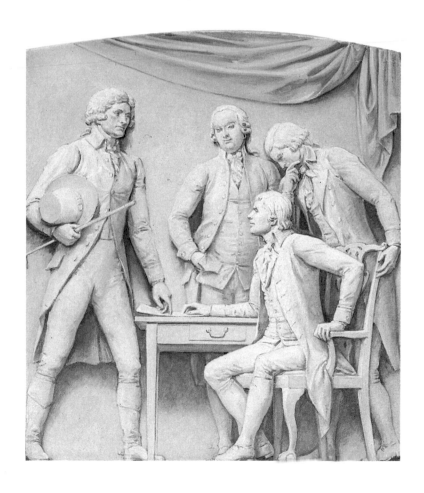

NATIONAL SOCIETY OF THE DAUGHTERS OF THE AMERICAN REVOLUTION

UNITED STATES CAPITOL HISTORICAL SOCIETY

CONTENTS

OFFICERS AND STAFF FOR THIS EDITION

Sarah M. King, *President General, National Society of the Daughters of the American Revolution*
Fred Schwengel, *President, United States Capitol Historical Society*
Robert L. Breeden, *Editorial Director*
Paul Martin, *Editor*
Cynthia B. Scudder, *Art Director*
Joseph H. Bailey, *Photographer*
Robert Schwengel, *Writer*
Richard Striner, *Historian*
Florian H. Thayn, *Art Researcher*
Robert W. Messer, *Production Manager*

Library of Congress Catalog Number 86-060792
ISBN 0-916200-07-8

Cover: *French-born architect and engineer Pierre Charles L'Enfant shows his plans for the new capital city to President George Washington in June 1791.* **Preceding page:** *Thomas Jefferson, left, presents a program for a competition for the design of the Capitol to federal commissioners Thomas Johnson, chairman (seated), David Stuart (behind chair), and Daniel Carroll (behind table).*

1969 landing on the moon in a mural in the Brumidi Corridor on the ground floor of the Senate wing.

Planning for the House wing murals began in the winter of 1969-70. The immediate challenge Cox faced was to design a series of compositions that would fit the varied shapes and spaces of the House wing corridors. It was decided to concentrate the murals on the corridors' vaulted ceilings, out of the way of the crowds that pass through these busy ground-floor hallways.

The artist first completed scale drawings of the proposed murals, making sure his designs harmonized with the architecture of Thomas U. Walter, designer of the House and Senate wings. Cox also made certain the murals would be historically accurate. He was aided by the staffs of the U.S. Capitol Historical Society, the Art and Reference Division of the Office of the Architect of the Capitol, the Library of Congress, the New York Historical Society, the Avery Library at Columbia University, the New York Public Library, and many local historical associations.

After his plans were approved, Cox began work in February 1973 in the north-south corridor leading to the House Restaurant, on the east side of the House wing. This first phase of work, funded by the U.S. Capitol Historical Society, is known as the Hall of Capitols. Among its subjects it includes paintings of all the buildings that have housed the U.S. Congress and its predecessors. At this stage of the project, Cox was joined by Clifford Young, an experienced muralist who helped work up the cartoons, or preparatory drawings, of the paintings. John Charles Roach also joined the staff. He would help paint many of the corridor's *trompe l'oeil* ornaments, classical decorations done in simulated relief.

After scaffolding was erected in the hallway, the plaster panels that would contain the murals were carefully repaired. Canvas

Designer of the Capitol Dr. William Thornton conceived an architectural plan of "grandeur" and "simplicity." Artist Constantino Brumidi painted in the Capitol from 1855 to 1880.

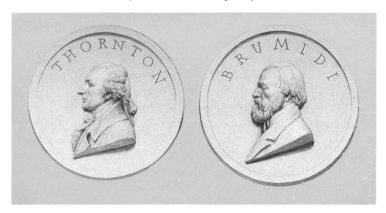

Allegorical figure representing Justice displays the trompe l'oeil, *or three-dimensional, effect achieved by muralist Cox.*

was then glued atop the plaster and a coat of white paint was applied as a base. Full-scale cartoons were transferred to the panels by "pouncing," applying powdered charcoal through perforated tracings of the drawings. This was followed by the actual painting, done in oil colors.

The first series of Cox murals was completed in July 1974. Two years later, as their contribution to the Bicentennial celebration, the Daughters of the American Revolution funded a second series of paintings, featuring 16 murals depicting the political, legislative, intellectual, and economic growth of the nation. These murals are in the central east-west corridor of the House wing, called Great Experiment Hall.

Cox and his associates completed this portion of the project in 1982, and it was dedicated in September of that year. Not long afterward, Allyn Cox died, but not before he had received a fitting tribute. On September 21, both houses of Congress honored him with a special recognition ceremony in Statuary Hall. Today, the work begun by this fine artist goes on. Plans and sketches have been completed for a third series of murals in the western north-south corridor of the House wing, and a possible fourth and final series of murals is being considered.

THE HALL OF CAPITOLS

COMPLETED IN 1974, the murals in the eastern north-south corridor of the House wing tell the story of the U.S. Capitol. Grouped in four panels are paintings of the 16 buildings in which Congress and its predecessors have met since 1754. Four other panels contain eight historical scenes set in or around the halls of Congress. Also included are 12 portraits of persons associated with the Capitol and a number of inscriptions and allegorical scenes. The diagram and key below gives the positions of the main paintings that make up the Hall of Capitols. (Note: Diagram shows murals as they appear overhead.) The murals are reproduced on the following 19 pages.

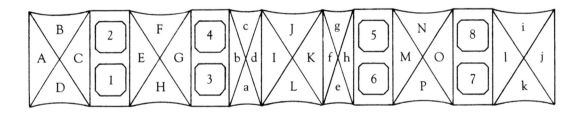

CAPITOLS

A Albany	I Trenton
B New York	J New York
C Philadelphia	K Philadelphia
D Philadelphia	L Washington
E Baltimore	M Washington
F York	N Washington
G Princeton	O Washington
H Annapolis	P Washington

SCENES

1 Burning of Capitol
2 Capitol as Hospital

3 Washington and L'Enfant
4 Laying Cornerstone

5 Jackson's Inaugural
6 Lincoln and Dome

7 Old House Chamber
8 Outer Lobby of House

PERSONS

a Latrobe	e Woods	i Trumball
b Bulfinch	f Lynn	j L'Enfant
c Walter	g Stewart	k Crawford
d Clark	h White	l Olmsted

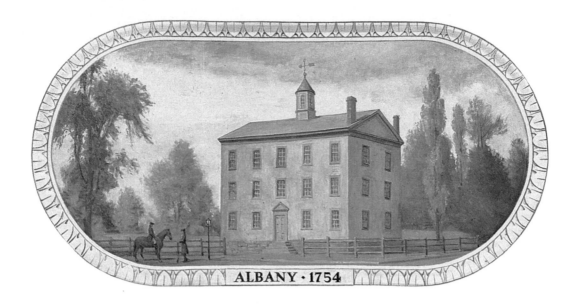

ALBANY · 1754

REPRESENTATIVES MEETING AT the old Stadt Huys in Albany, New York, developed the first plan for a union of the colonies. Though rejected, the plan became a guide for later federation.

DELEGATES FROM NINE COLONIES gathered in New York's old City Hall in response to the Stamp Act, a tax imposed by Great Britain. The delegates drew up a Declaration of Rights.

NEW YORK · 1765

PHILADELPHIA · 1774

CARPENTERS HALL IN PHILADELPHIA served as the site of the First Continental Congress, at which representatives from all 13 colonies agreed to suspend trade with Great Britain.

THE SECOND CONTINENTAL CONGRESS met in Philadephia's State House. Since July 4, 1776, when delegates issued a Declaration of Independence, the building has been called Independence Hall.

PHILADELPHIA · 1775

BRITISH BURN THE CAPITOL · 1814

EARLY IN OUR NATION'S HISTORY, Great Britain provoked the United States by interfering with international trade and impressing American seamen. After heated debates in Congress, war was declared against the British on June 18, 1812. The young government, however, was not completely prepared for what followed.

In the summer of 1814, Rear Adm. Sir George Cockburn landed troops on Maryland's Patuxent shore. A small group of defenders met the British near Bladensburg, but they were easily defeated. On August 24, the British captured Washington and set fire to most of its public buildings. The mural depicts the British on the west side of the Capitol. The building was gutted and would probably have been destroyed had not a rainstorm struck that night. The next day, the invaders withdrew, shaken by an accidental explosion, a violent windstorm, and a rumor that American troops were gathering outside the city.

Congress managed to carry on its business despite the destruction, meeting briefly in the Patent Office building, the only government office building not set afire by the British. From 1815 to 1819, while the permanent Capitol was being rebuilt, Congress met in the structure known as the Brick Capitol.

ROTUNDA DURING CIVIL WAR · 1862

DURING THE EARLY DAYS of the Civil War, an incoming flood of Union soldiers and armaments turned Washington into a fortified city. By order of President Abraham Lincoln and the War Department, the Capitol building was converted into a support facility for military personnel stationed in or near Washington. The Capitol initially served as a barracks for some 3,000 soldiers, and also as a bakery that supplied bread for troops manning the city's fortifications.

By the autumn of 1862, the war had come uncomfortably close to Washington, and for about six weeks, the Capitol was used as an emergency hospital. Some 1,500 cots were set up in the Capitol's hallways and chambers. Here were brought casualties from the battles of Second Manassas and Antietam.

The mural shows wounded soldiers being attended to inside the Rotunda. The scaffold at right was part of the construction work then underway on the Capitol's unfinished Dome. Nurses such as Dorothea Dix and future American Red Cross founder Clara Barton served here during this time. Also comforting the sick and dying soldiers was the poet Walt Whitman, shown sitting by a soldier's bed to the right of the door at left.

BALTIMORE · 1776

BRITISH VICTORIES AFTER the Declaration of Independence forced Congress to move from Philadelphia to Baltimore, where it met in a rented building since known as Congress House.

FOLLOWING ITS STAY in Baltimore, Congress returned briefly to Philadelphia, but was soon forced to move to York, Pennsylvania. There it met for nine months in the old Court House.

YORK, PA · 1777

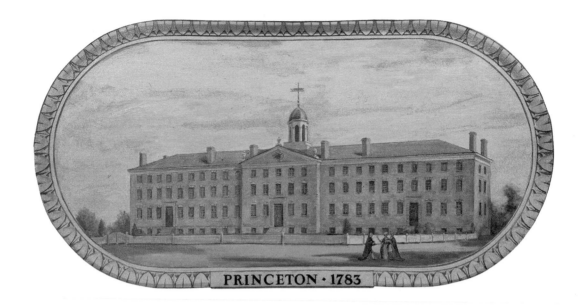

PRINCETON · 1783

IN THE SUMMER OF 1783, Congress met in Nassau Hall in Princeton, New Jersey. A few years earlier, General Washington had driven the British from this same building.

FROM PRINCETON, CONGRESS adjourned to Annapolis, Maryland, where it met in the State House. Here Washington later resigned as commander in chief of the Continental Army.

ANNAPOLIS · 1783

ON JULY 16, 1790, CONGRESS chose the permanent seat of the new federal government. It selected a hundred-square-mile plot along the Potomac River recommended by President Washington. Congress settled on this location because, among other things, it was accessible to northern and southern states and could conveniently receive overland and water transport.

Charged with planning the capital, President Washington chose French-born architect and engineer Pierre Charles L'Enfant as his advisor. Here L'Enfant shows Washington his plans for the city as they inspect the area in June 1791. Influenced by the design of Paris, L'Enfant laid out streets and helped select the sites for the home of Congress and for the President's "palace." The Capitol would be built on a site known as Jenkins' Hill, "a pedestal waiting for a monument" as L'Enfant called it.

A broad thoroughfare—today's Pennsylvania Avenue—was to connect the Capitol and the presidential residence. L'Enfant's plan called for the streets of Washington to radiate from the Capitol like the spokes of a wheel. To obtain a design for the Capitol building, the federal commissioners held a competition, awarding the winner, Dr. William Thornton, $500 and a city lot.

CAPITOL SITE SELECTION · 1791

ON SEPTEMBER 18, 1793, a procession led by President Washington set off from the Virginia side of the "Grand River Potowmack," crossed to the Maryland side, and proceeded to President's Square in the District of Columbia. Included were members of the Masonic lodges of Virginia, Maryland, and the District. "The procession marched two abreast," reported the *Alexandria Gazette*, "in the greatest solemn dignity, with music playing, drums beating, colours flying and spectators rejoicing."

From President's Square, the group marched toward the hilltop site of the new Capitol, breaking ranks to cross a log over Tiber Creek at the foot of the hill. Arriving at the site, George Washington laid the cornerstone of the new Capitol. He appears here in the sash, collar, and apron of the Masonic order.

A silver plate beneath the cornerstone marks the date as the 13th year of American independence, first year of Washington's second term, and the year of Masonry 5793. The ceremony ended with prayer, Masonic chanting honors, and a volley from the Alexandria Volunteer Artillery. Today, although the location of the cornerstone is uncertain, its approximate site is marked by a bronze plaque on the Senate wing's central East Front entrance.

CAPITOL CORNERSTONE CEREMONY · 1793

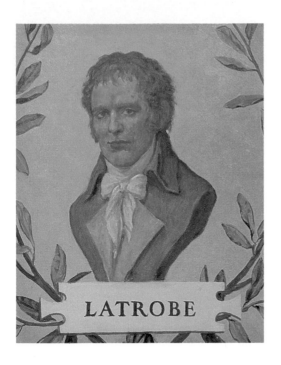

Eight men have served as Architect of the Capitol following William Thornton, the original designer. Benjamin H. Latrobe (1803-11, 1815-17) built the original House wing; Charles Bulfinch (1818-29) constructed the center section and first Dome; Thomas U. Walter (1851-65) built the present Dome and extended the North and South Wings; Edward Clark (1865-1902)

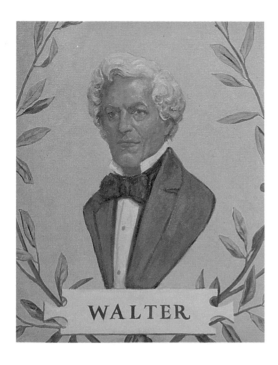

WOODS

LYNN

completed the porticoes of the new wings; Elliott Woods (1902-23) erected the first House and Senate Office Buildings; David Lynn (1923-54) constructed the Longworth House Office and Supreme Court Buildings; J. George Stewart (1954-70) extended the East Front; George M. White (1971-) constructed the Madison Memorial Library of Congress Building.

STEWART

WHITE

TRENTON · 1784

In 1784, CONGRESS MET for a month in the French Arms Tavern in Trenton, New Jersey. Three years later, the Constitution was read to the nation from the old Court House across the street.

TWENTY YEARS AFTER first meeting there, Congress gathered in New York's old City Hall. In 1789, Washington was inaugurated here and the first Congress convened under the Constitution.

NEW YORK · 1785

PHILADELPHIA · 1790

THE FEDERAL CONGRESS moved back to Philadelphia in 1790, this time to Congress Hall. It remained in session here for the next ten years while a permanent Capitol was built in Washington.

BY 1800, THE NORTH WING of the new Capitol was completed. George Washington, who died in 1799, neither presided in the city that bears his name nor saw the finished Capitol.

WASHINGTON · 1800

FIRST CAPITOL INAUGURATION · 1829

UNTIL THE ELECTION OF Andrew Jackson of Tennessee as President, most new chief executives were installed in office in either the Senate or House Chambers, with only special guests in attendance. Viewing himself as a man of the people, "Old Hickory" was determined to be sworn into office in public.

On March 4, 1829, hundreds of anxious well-wishers and supporters gathered on the Capitol grounds to view the inauguration. Jackson vetoed a military pageant and simply walked from Gadsby's Hotel to the Capitol through the crowd of cheering people. The mural shows Jackson being sworn in on the East Front portico by Chief Justice John Marshall. Since that day, East Front inaugural ceremonies have been a tradition, though in 1981 Ronald Reagan was sworn in on the West Front.

After Jackson's inauguration, there was to be a reception at the White House for special guests. However, tables of food and drink that had been laid out in the East Room were mobbed by an unexpected crowd that pushed its way into the private reception. The crowd was persuaded to leave only when Jackson returned to Gadsby's Hotel and tubs of punch were placed on the White House lawn.

NEW DOME SYMBOLIZES UNION · 1863

In March of 1855, Congress authorized the construction of a new Dome for the Capitol to complement the enlarged House and Senate wings. The Dome was designed by Thomas U. Walter, Architect of the Capitol from 1851 to 1865. The mural depicts Walter, at right, showing his plans to President Lincoln.

Work on the Dome was temporarily interrupted by the Civil War, but in October 1862, Lincoln ordered that work be continued as "a sign we intend the Union shall go on." The construction of the nine-million-pound cast-iron Dome is considered a masterpiece of 19th-century engineering. Its inner and outer shells expand or contract in response to the weather. Between the shells, a stairway of 183 steps leads to the top of the Dome.

Crowning the Dome is the 19 1/2-foot bronze statue designed by Thomas Crawford. The allegorical figure "Freedom" is of a helmeted woman with one hand holding a sword and the other hand holding a wreath and resting on a shield. The statue was hoisted to the top of the Dome in five sections, the last on December 2, 1863. The U.S. flag was then unfurled, and a 35-gun salute—one for each state in the Union, northern and southern—echoed across Capitol Hill.

WASHINGTON · 1814

In 1814, the Capitol was set afire by the British. Congress met that fall in the Patent Office building, the only government office building in Washington that was not burned.

While the devastation of 1814 was being repaired, Congress convened in a temporary structure known as the Brick Capitol. Not until 1819 did it move back into the permanent Capitol.

WASHINGTON 1815

WASHINGTON · 1829

REPAIRS TO THE CAPITOL were completed by architect Charles Bulfinch. He also finished the building's central portion, including a Rotunda covered by a copper-sheathed wooden dome.

By 1867, THE CAPITOL had taken its modern form. Under the direction of Thomas U. Walter, the North and South Wings were built and an enlarged Dome replaced the Bulfinch Dome.

WASHINGTON 1867

THE OLD HALL OF THE HOUSE was designed by Architect of the Capitol Benjamin Henry Latrobe following the devasting fire set by the British in 1814. Although Latrobe's semicircular design was opposed by the Capitol's original architect, Dr. William Thornton, Congress accepted the plan. Featured in the chamber were columns cut from quarries in Loudoun County, Virginia, and Montgomery County, Maryland. Red draperies were hung between the columns to dampen echoes in the chamber.

Shown speaking in the Hall of the House is John Quincy Adams, near the center with hand raised. Adams is the only man elected to the House of Representatives after serving as President. Seated under the canopy at left is Speaker of the House James K. Polk, who later became the nation's 11th President.

The House held sessions in this room until 1857, when it moved into its present, larger chambers. In 1864, Congress invited each state to present the Capitol with statues of two of its honored citizens. Forty such statues stand in the old House Chamber, today known as Statuary Hall. The hall was restored to its 1857 appearance in time for the Bicentennial. Even its red draperies were recreated from a swatch of original material.

OLD HOUSE CHAMBER · 1838

IN 1866, CONGRESS DEBATED a civil rights bill that would overturn Southern "black codes" limiting the rights of blacks. A forerunner of the 14th Amendment, the bill provided that there be no discrimination on account of race or previous condition of slavery. The mural depicts a scene at that time outside the House of Representatives. The outer lobby was a typical place for conversation between legislators and citizens with special interests, or "lobbyists," as they came to be called.

In the foreground are two famous civil rights defenders, Henry Garnet, left, and Horace Greeley. Garnet was born a slave but earned freedom in 1826. He was educated at Oneida Institute in New York and then became a leading abolitionist. Greeley was the founder and editor of the *New York Tribune*, whose editorials greatly influenced public opinion. At the time of this debate, Greeley was a supporter of Negro suffrage and Southern amnesty. In the background of the mural are the bronze doors modeled by Randolph Rogers. The doors opened into this House corridor for several years. Eventually it was decided that, because of their beauty, the doors should have greater prominence. In 1871 they were moved to the Rotunda entrance.

CIVIL RIGHTS BILL PASSES · 1866

TRUMBULL

L ENFANT

AMONG THE OUTSTANDING FIGURES associated with the Capitol
are John Trumbull, whose paintings of the Revolution now hang
in the Capitol Rotunda; Pierre L'Enfant, planner of the capital
city; Thomas Crawford, whose bronze statue, "Freedom," crowns
the Capitol Dome; and landscape architect Frederick Law Olmsted, who refined the Capitol grounds in the latter 1800s.

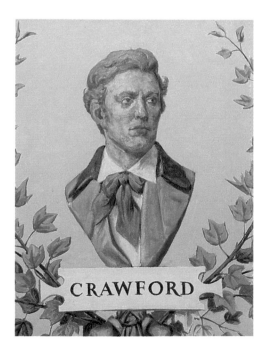

CRAWFORD

OLMSTED

GREAT EXPERIMENT HALL

DEDICATED IN 1982, the second series of Allyn Cox murals occupies the central east-west corridor of the House wing. Intersecting with the Hall of Capitols, this corridor is known as Great Experiment Hall. In 16 major paintings, it depicts the growth of the American experiment in democracy and free enterprise. Each scene is amplified by vignettes relating to the historical theme. The murals also feature several portraits of notable Americans and a number of inscriptions and allegorical paintings. The diagram and key below gives the positions of the main elements. (Note: Diagram shows murals as they appear overhead.) The next 19 pages present the murals.

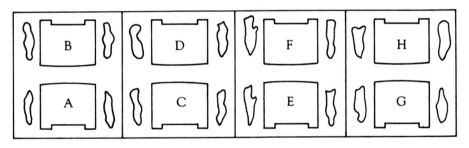

A Mayflower Compact
B Albany Congress

C First Continental Congress
D Writing the Declaration

E Planning the Constitution
F First Federal Congress

G Washington's Inaugural
H Washington's Farewell

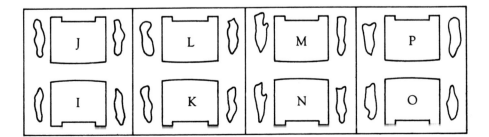

I Monroe Doctrine
J Lincoln's Second Inaugural

K Smithsonian Institution
L Old Library of Congress

M Evan's Steam Dredger
N Nashua Iron Company

O Roosevelt Speaks
P Women's Franchise

FREEDOM OF SPEECH

LOCATED AT THE EAST END of Great Experiment Hall are allegorical figures representing the Four Freedoms enunciated by President Franklin D. Roosevelt in his message to Congress of 1941.

FREEDOM FROM FEAR

FREEDOM FROM WANT

FREEDOM OF RELIGION

THE MAYFLOWER COMPACT · 1620

THE ALBANY CONGRESS · 1754

On November 21, 1620, a small group of men and women signed a landmark document aboard the sailing ship *Mayflower*. The document called for "a civill body politick" to frame "just and equall lawes" in the New World colony soon to be established by the Pilgrim passengers. The Mayflower Compact thus set forth the principles of tolerance and liberty that would be proclaimed in the Declaration of Independence 156 years later.

Shown signing the historic document in the cabin of the *Mayflower* is Pilgrim leader William Brewster. Standing at left is the colony's military leader, Capt. Miles Standish. In all, 41 adults added their names to the Mayflower Compact.

Landing at Plymouth in December, the Pilgrims set about building a settlement in the wilderness. In the vignette at right, a Pilgrim spins in front of a typical house built of sticks and clay. Though the first winter was mild, half the 101 settlers died from disease. Their hard beginnings taught them the necessity of seeking help, so they formed friendships with the Indians, represented by the vignette at left.

After their first harvest, in the fall of 1621, the Pilgrims invited the Indians to join them in a day of thanksgiving. That humble celebration set the precedent for the holiday still observed by Americans on the fourth Thursday in November.

In 1754, the British government called for a meeting of colonial representatives at Albany, New York. The purpose was to work out a treaty with the Indians and to make plans for the defense of the colonies against the French. The meeting, however, was to have far greater impact. Discussions at Albany led to the first plan for a federal government of the colonies.

The mural depicts some of those present. At left are William Franklin and his father, Benjamin, of Pennsylvania. To the right are Governor Thomas Hutchinson of Massachusetts, Governor William Delancey of New York, Sir William Johnson of Massachusetts, and Col. Benjamin Tasker of Maryland. The vignettes at left and right represent trades and farming of the period.

The plan adopted at Albany was one proposed by Benjamin Franklin. It called for a President General to be appointed by the Crown and a Grand Council of Delegates from the colonial assemblies. The council was to be empowered to levy taxes, engage and pay soldiers, and build forts and equip vessels.

The royal government disapproved of the plan because it encroached on the Crown's prerogative. Even the colonies rejected it, believing it infringed on their independence. Despite its rejection, the Albany Plan proved a valuable guide to the union of the colonies in the years leading to independence.

THE FIRST CONTINENTAL CONGRESS · 1774

WHEN GREAT BRITAIN ATTEMPTED to tighten its control of the colonies after the French and Indian War, many colonists protested. One protest in 1773—the Boston Tea Party—led Parliament to close the port of Boston and virtually abolish provincial self-government in Massachusetts.

In the summer of 1774, the Massachusetts Assembly responded by inviting all 13 colonies to send delegates to a convention to discuss ways of resisting Great Britain. British occupation, depicted in the vignette at right, and taxation without representation, in the vignette at left, were two of the colonies' complaints against the royal government.

Fifty-six delegates assembled that September in Philadelphia's Carpenters Hall. After weeks of debate, such as the stirring oration by Patrick Henry shown here, the First Continental Congress formally declared that American colonists were entitled to the same rights as Englishmen. The delegates also agreed to form the Continental Association, which called for the suspension of trade with Great Britain.

Upon adjourning in late October, the delegates resolved to reconvene in May of 1775 if the British had not met their demands. Thus the stage was set for the Second Continental Congress and the Declaration of Independence.

THE DECLARATION OF INDEPENDENCE · 1776

TREMENDOUS COURAGE WAS CALLED FOR when five Americans met in Philadelphia in June 1776 to draft a Declaration of Independence. Depicted here, from the left, Benjamin Franklin, Roger Sherman, Thomas Jefferson, Robert Livingston, and John Adams all faced the possibility of being shot as traitors had the British discovered their act of defiance.

The philosophy of the document these men produced was inspired by John Locke, whose portrait hangs behind the framers. In his *Second Essay on Government*, Locke proclaimed that the rights of man include the right of revolution.

Thomas Jefferson was the principal author of the Declaration. Citing a long list of reasons for independence, Jefferson wrote that man's "unalienable Rights" include "Life, Liberty, and the Pursuit of Happiness." The framers of the Declaration presented their work to the Second Continental Congress. After a number of changes, the document that has become a nation's symbol of liberty was adopted on July 2 and signed on July 4.

The vignettes that accompany the mural show two famous American patriots. On the left is John Paul Jones hoisting the Continental Colors, the first national flag of the United States. At right is George Washington portrayed on the only occasion he wore the uniform of a British officer.

By the mid-1780s, weaknesses were evident in the Articles of Confederation, under which the federal government had been formed. The inability to levy taxes or to regulate interstate commerce and foreign policy severely handicapped the government.

In 1787, a Constitutional Convention was called to amend the Articles of Confederation. Meeting in Philadelphia from May 25 to September 17, 55 delegates debated, and 39 signed, the new Constitution. The delegates included many leading men. In the mural, four leaders meet in the garden of Benjamin Franklin. They are, from left, Alexander Hamilton, James Wilson, James Madison, and Franklin. The vignettes symbolize concerns of the time: education for all, left, and freedom from search, right.

The drafters of the Constitution sought to insure that the tyranny experienced under British rule would not occur under our own government. Two key provisions of the Constitution were aimed at preventing governmental abuses—the separation of powers and the system of checks and balances.

The document the delegates produced created a strong central government, yet one that is responsive to the desires of the people. Since its ratification in 1788, the U.S. Constitution has proved to be a living document, one adaptable to changing times through judicial review and the amendment process.

The first federal Congress, instituted by Article I of the Constitution, met in New York City's Federal Hall on March 4, 1789. The House of Representatives was presided over by Speaker Frederick Muhlenberg, shown seated in the mural. Standing at left is James Madison. Standing on the right are Elbridge Gerry, foreground, and Fisher Ames, at rear. Both the House and Senate devoted much attention to the details of organizing the government under the new Constitution. Each body was granted certain powers, but how these powers would be exercised depended on the members of this first Congress.

The first Congress made several invaluable contributions to legislative history. The committee system was initiated, and the Senate exercised its powers of advice and consent. Taxes and imposts were levied, and a judicial system was enacted. Its most important achievement was the passage of the Bill of Rights.

At the insistence of James Madison, the House of Representatives recommended for adoption 12 amendments guaranteeing certain rights to states and to individuals. Ten of the amendments were ratified by the states. These first ten amendments to the Constitution assure Americans of such inalienable rights as freedom of religion, represented by the vignette at left, and freedom of the press, symbolized by the vignette at right.

THE CONSTITUTIONAL CONVENTION · 1787

THE FIRST FEDERAL CONGRESS · 1789

IN APRIL 1789, BALLOTS FOR the election of the nation's first President were counted by Congress in New York City. George Washington was elected President and John Adams was elected Vice President. At the time, Washington was at Mount Vernon, in Virginia. His week-long journey from his home to New York was a triumphal tour. Along the way, tumultuous crowds greeted the austere, dignified hero of the Revolution.

On April 30, Washington was sworn into office on the balcony of Federal Hall. Shown administering the oath of office is Robert R. Livingston, chancellor of the State of New York. Vice President Adams looks on to the right of Washington. Holding the Bible is Samuel Otis, Secretary of the Senate. The two vignettes represent milestone achievements of the new government, the establishment of a judicial system, at left, and the beginning of a national banking system, at right.

After being sworn in, Washington returned to the Senate Chamber to deliver his inaugural address. According to one observer, he was agitated and embarrassed. "He trembled, and several times could scarce make out to read." He spoke of his "conflict of emotions"—the clash between his love of country and his recognition of his own inadequacies. Yet he pledged to serve and to seek that divine guidance he saw leading the United States.

WASHINGTON'S INAUGURATION · 1789

AT THE END OF HIS SECOND TERM of office, President Washington issued a farewell address. The address first appeared in the pages of the Philadelphia *Daily American Advertiser* on September 19, 1796. The mural shows Washington writing his address with the help of Alexander Hamilton.

In his address, the President warned the country against permanent alliances with foreign powers. Washington believed that for America to flourish it must "Observe good faith and justice toward all nations. Cultivate peace and harmony with all." The sawyer in the vignette at left and the sailing ships at right symbolize the growing importance of American commerce with foreign countries.

Washington also warned the American people against incurring a large public debt or against maintaining a large military establishment. And he cautioned against the devices of a "small, artful, enterprising minority" to manipulate government.

Since it was written, Washington's Farewell Address has been reprinted thousands of times. Each year, on the day nearest Washington's birthday, the address is read in the U.S. Senate— reminding our present leaders that "Of all the dispositions and habits which lead to political prosperity, religion and morality are indispensable supports."

WASHINGTON'S FAREWELL ADDRESS · 1796

THE MONROE DOCTRINE · 1823

LINCOLN'S SECOND INAUGURAL · 1865

IN 1823, OUR FIFTH PRESIDENT, James Monroe, faced a pair of diplomatic difficulties. Two years earlier, the Russian Czar had extended his country's claims along the northern Pacific coast from Alaska to Oregon. In addition, the United States was concerned that European powers would try to regain control of the Latin American states that had recently revolted from Spain.

At the urging of Secretary of State John Quincy Adams, Monroe announced a sweeping new U.S. policy, which came to be called the Monroe Doctrine. Issued in Monroe's annual message to Congress on December 2, the Monroe Doctrine set forth two bold assertions—that no new colonization would be allowed in the Americas, and that European powers were not to interfere in the affairs of this hemisphere. Though these were beyond our power to enforce at the time, they expressed a principle that remains a cornerstone of U.S. foreign policy.

The mural shows President Monroe, at left, and the members of his Cabinet as they discuss the new policy. Standing at the globe is Secretary of State Adams. To the right are Attorney General William Wirt, Secretary of War John Calhoun, and Secretary of the Navy Samuel L. Southard. The vignettes depict struggles of liberation, represented by South American hero Simon Bolivar, at left, and Greek freedom fighters, at right.

THE CIVIL WAR WAS DRAWING to a close when Abraham Lincoln took the oath of office for his second term on the steps of the newly completed Capitol. For months the President's thoughts had been directed toward the reconstruction of the Union. He realized many Northerners wished revenge, hoping to totally overhaul the South's political, economic, and social structures. The President argued for a more moderate approach, on the grounds that the seceded states had never legally left the Union.

Vice President Andrew Johnson, depicted to the left of Lincoln, and Chief Justice Salmon P. Chase, on the right, listened along with the others present on March 4, 1865, as the President delivered his Second Inaugural Address. Imbued with biblical allusions, Lincoln's address was a plea for humility and humanity:

"With malice toward none; with charity for all; with firmness in the right, as God gives us to see the right, let us strive on to finish the work we are in; to bind up the nation's wounds; to care for him who shall have borne the battle, and for his widow, and his orphan—to do all which may achieve and cherish a just and lasting peace among ourselves, and with all nations."

The soldier in the vignette at left stands for a nation reunited. In the vignette at right, an emancipated black exercises his newly won right to vote.

THE SMITHSONIAN INSTITUTION · 1855

THIS NATION'S FINEST COMPLEX of public museums, the Smithsonian Institution, exists thanks to an unexpected gift from an English scientist. James Smithson, who was born in France in 1765, never saw the United States or wrote to anyone living here. Yet he left a fortune to found an American establishment "for the increase and diffusion of knowledge among men."

When Smithson was born, he was christened James Lewis Macie. His mother, Elizabeth Macie, had been widowed before her son's birth. James' blood father was Hugh Smithson Percy, a wealthy Englishman who was later knighted as the Duke of Northumberland. While in college, young Macie signed his papers James Smithson, keeping that name for the rest of his life. On his death in 1829, his estate of $550,000 was bequeathed to the United States. Seventeen years later Congress accepted the bequest, and in 1846 the Smithsonian Institution was founded.

In 1855, the famous red sandstone "Castle," depicted in the mural, opened its doors. The two vignettes capture the spirit of exploration and discovery the Smithsonian represents. At left, American author John Lloyd Stephens and English illustrator Frederick Catherwood explore Central American ruins in 1839. At right, Charles Willson Peale excavates a mastodon skeleton near Newburg, Pennsylvania, in 1802.

THE IDEA FOR A LIBRARY OF CONGRESS was initiated by James Madison. His service in Congress convinced him that legislators needed to be better informed. He believed Congress should have convenient access to works on the law of nations. And he felt "no time ought to be lost in collecting every book and tract relating to American antiquities and affairs." In January 1783, he introduced a resolution to create a library to meet those needs.

In 1800, the Library of Congress was founded and given one room in the Capitol. The mural shows the library in 1890. Seated at left is Ainsworth Spofford, Librarian of Congress. The vignettes represent education in America in the 1800s. At left, a schoolmarm teaches youngsters in a "little red schoolhouse." At right, students attend a land grant college.

In 1897, the library moved to its own building, now named in honor of Thomas Jefferson. The original building and two others, named for John Adams and James Madison, make up today's main library complex. Representing more than 450 languages, the library's holdings total some 80 million items. Its collection covers virtually every subject known to man and includes all types of documents, from papyrus to microfilm. In addition to meeting the needs of Congress, the facility serves the executive branch, the courts, and scholars from all over the world.

ALTHOUGH STEAM ENGINES WERE in use in the 1700s, early engines were too heavy and inefficient for practical use in powering land vehicles or boats. By 1802, however, American inventor Oliver Evans developed a high-pressure steam engine that produced more power and weighed far less than earlier models.

In 1804, Evans used his engine in the first steam-powered dredging scow. The amphibious dredger had both a paddle and rollers, so it could move under its own power on water or land. The mural shows his dredger at work on the Schuylkill River. Evans is seated at right in the back.

Subsequent breakthroughs in land and water travel were made possible by the pioneering work of this little-known inventor. The vignettes accompanying the mural depict two 19th century achievements in travel. At left is a steamboat on the Platte River. In the 1800s, steamboats carried people and goods on many inland rivers, a key to opening the nation's heartland.

At right, the world's first railroad suspension bridge spans the Niagara River near Niagara Falls. Designed by John Augustus Roebling, the bridge was completed in 1855. In 1867, Roebling was named chief engineer of the Brooklyn Bridge. At the time of its completion, the Brooklyn Bridge ranked as the world's longest, with a main span of 1,595 feet.

IRON AND STEEL FORMED THE BACKBONE of America's industrial revolution of the 19th century. The manufacturing of everything from railroads to stoves to skyscrapers depended on iron or steel. The first attempt at iron-making in America was made in Virginia shortly after the colony was established.

Rapid development of the industry began in the 1720s, and by 1775, there were more blast furnaces and forges in the colonies than in England and Wales combined. The process of iron-making did not change much until the 19th century, when anthracite and coke were substituted for charcoal as fuels.

After the Civil War, iron gave way to steel. Leading the industry were men such as Andrew Carnegie. Better manufacturing techniques, such as the Bessemer and open-hearth processes, made it possible to make steel economically and in large quantities. The first American plant to take advantage of such techniques opened in Michigan in 1864. Ingots produced there were rolled into the first steel rails made in America.

The mural shows men at work in the Nashua, New Hampshire, Iron Company. The vignettes depict changes in American society brought about by industrialization and mechanization. On the left, women leave the home to go to work in a factory. At right, hand labor in the South gives way to the cotton gin.

STEAM POWERED AMPHIBIOUS BOAT · 1804

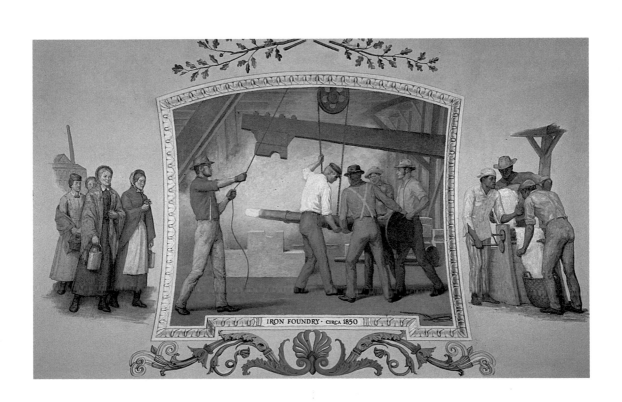

IRON FOUNDRY · CIRCA 1850

THEODORE ROOSEVELT, OUR NATION's 26th President, is remembered for many things, not the least of which was his rousing style of public speaking. In the mural, Roosevelt makes a point with fist-pounding enthusiasm. Taking notes in the foreground, at right, is the famous writer and editor, H.L. Mencken.

Roosevelt came into office in 1901, a time when trusts and monopolies held sway over the national economy. Roosevelt championed the cause of the little man, denounced "malefactors of great wealth," and engaged in "trust-busting" under the terms of the Sherman Antitrust Act. In addition to his efforts to regulate big business, the President did much to strengthen the nation's role in international affairs. One lasting contribution he worked for was the building of a canal through the Isthmus of Panama. The vignette at left shows the digging of the canal, which was opened to international sea traffic on August 15, 1914.

At home, Roosevelt made an enduring contribution to America's future through his leadership in developing conservation programs. During his administration, more than 234 million acres of land were acquired for the public domain. In pursuing his conservation policies, Roosevelt was aided immensely by the chief of the Forest Service—and America's first professional forester—Gifford Pinchot, shown in the vignette at right.

THEODORE ROOSEVELT · CIRCA 1904

THE BATTLE TO EXTEND THE FRANCHISE to women was a long one. In March of 1776, Abigail Adams wrote her husband, John, then sitting with the Continental Congress: "If perticuliar care and attention is not paid to the Laidies we are determined to foment a Rebelion, and will not hold ourselves bound by any Laws in which we have no voice, or Representation."

Three-quarters of a century later women still were without franchise. That situation led Elizabeth Cady Stanton to organize the first women's rights convention, held in 1848 in Seneca Falls, New York. Other leaders of that period included Susan B. Anthony and Lucretia Mott. Their struggle had to be carried into the next century. In 1917, Anna Howard Shaw, shown here in cap and gown, led a suffrage parade in New York. A licensed minister and physician, she was a prominent lecturer on women's rights. Marching at right is Carrie Chapman Catt, president of the National American Woman Suffrage Association.

The determined efforts of such individuals paid dividends in 1920. In that year, the ratification of the 19th Amendment gave nationwide suffrage to women. In the vignette at left is Montana's Jeannette Rankin, in 1917 the first woman member of the U.S. House of Representatives. At right is the first black congressman, South Carolina's Joseph H. Rainey, elected in 1870.

WOMEN'S SUFFRAGE PARADE · 1917

Allegorical figure of History Turning the Page concludes Great Experiment Hall, finished not long before the death of Allyn Cox.

Throughout the House wing murals are a number of inscriptions selected by the artist. Those below appear in the Hall of Capitols. Those opposite are from Great Experiment Hall.

This government
the offspring of our own choice
uninfluenced and unawed
has a just claim
to your confidence & support

GEORGE WASHINGTON

Man is not made for the state
but the state for man
and it derives its just powers
only from the consent
of the governed

THOMAS JEFFERSON

You are the rulers
and the ruled

ADLAI E. STEVENSON

One country
one Constitution
one destiny

DANIEL WEBSTER

Liberty and union
one and inseparable

DANIEL WEBSTER

We have built no temple
but the Capitol
We consult no common oracle
but the Constitution

RUFUS CHOATE

Here sir the people govern

ALEXANDER HAMILTON

The only legitimate right to govern
is an express grant of power
from the governed

WILLIAM HENRY HARRISON

Whenever a people or an institution
forgets its hard beginnings
it is beginning to decay

CARL SANDBURG

Our government
conceived in freedom
and purchased with blood
can be preserved only by constant vigilance

WILLIAM JENNINGS BRYAN

I have but one lamp
by which my feet are guided
and that is the lamp
of experience

PATRICK HENRY

When tillage begins
other arts follow
The farmers therefore
are the founders of human civilization

DANIEL WEBSTER

Without freedom of thought
there can be no such thing as wisdom
& no such thing as publick liberty
without freedom of speech

BENJAMIN FRANKLIN

Let us build broad and wide
these foundations
Let them abut only
on the everlasting seas

IGNATIUS DONNELLY

The greatest dangers to liberty
lurk in insidious encroachment
by men of zeal
well-meaning but without understanding

LOUIS D. BRANDEIS

We must remember that any oppression
any injustice any hatred is a wedge
designed to attack our civilization

FRANKLIN DELANO ROOSEVELT

Wherever a free man is in chains
we are threatened also
Whoever is fighting for liberty
is defending America

WILLIAM ALLEN WHITE

Freedom of thought
and the right of private judgment
in matters of conscience
direct their course to this happy country

SAMUEL ADAMS

We defend and we build
a way of life
not for America alone
but for all mankind

FRANKLIN DELANO ROOSEVELT

Labor is discovered
to be the grand conqueror
enriching and building up nations
more surely than the proudest battles

WILLIAM ELLERY CHANNING

He that invents a machine
augments the power of man
and the well-being of mankind

HENRY WARD BEECHER

The nation behaves well if it treats
the natural resources as assets
which it must turn over
to the next generation
increased and not impaired in value

THEODORE ROOSEVELT

Enlighten the people generally
and tyranny and oppressions
of body and mind will vanish
like evil spirits at the dawn of day

THOMAS JEFFERSON

A CONTINUING
PROJECT

COMPLEMENTING THE HALL OF CAPITOLS and Great Experiment Hall will be a third series of murals, on the theme of America's westward expansion. Plans and sketches have been completed for the murals, which will be located in the western north-south corridor of the House wing. The murals will include maps and scenes showing the United States' growth through the acquistion of Alaska and Hawaii. The color drawing below shows the planned layout of the murals. In addition to this project, a final fourth series of murals is being considered.

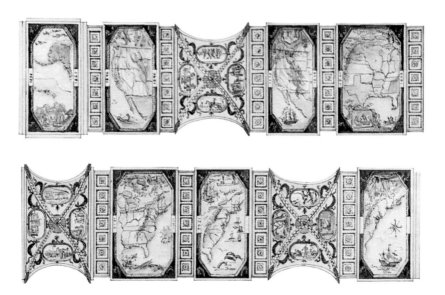